THE SPIRIT WITHIN

"WHAT ARE YOU MADE OF"?

JAMES FLOYD

authorHOUSE

AuthorHouse™
1663 Liberty Drive
Bloomington, IN 47403
www.authorhouse.com
Phone: 833-262-8899

© 2021 James Floyd. All rights reserved.

No part of this book may be reproduced, stored in a retrieval system, or transmitted by any means without the written permission of the author.

Published by AuthorHouse 02/24/2021

ISBN: 978-1-6655-1785-0 (sc)
ISBN: 978-1-6655-1783-6 (hc)
ISBN: 978-1-6655-1784-3 (e)

Library of Congress Control Number: 2021903664

Print information available on the last page.

Any people depicted in stock imagery provided by Getty Images are models, and such images are being used for illustrative purposes only.
Certain stock imagery © Getty Images.

New International Version (NIV) Holy Bible, New International Version®, NIV® Copyright ©1973, 1978, 1984, 2011 by Biblica, Inc.® Used by permission

New Living Translation (NLT) Holy Bible, New Living Translation, copyright © 1996, 2004, 2015 by Tyndale House Foundation. Used by permission of Tyndale House Publishers, Inc., Carol Stream, Illinois 60188. All rights reserved

English Standard Version (ESV) The Holy Bible, English Standard Version. ESV® Text Edition: 2016. Copyright © 2001 by Crossway Bibles, a publishing ministry of Good News Publishers

King James Version. Public Domain.

This book is printed on acid-free paper.

Because of the dynamic nature of the Internet, any web addresses or links contained in this book may have changed since publication and may no longer be valid. The views expressed in this work are solely those of the author and do not necessarily reflect the views of the publisher, and the publisher hereby disclaims any responsibility for them.

ACKNOWLEDGEMENT

I first want to begin by thanking God for all the blessings that he brought into my life. I want to thank him for continuing to see the best in me when so many were planning and hoping for my destruction. God truly has been good to me and I thank him for giving the inspiration to try and inspire others.

I want to thank my dear friend, classmate, and colleague Donna Marie Mandigo of Donna Marie Photo Company for an awesome photo cover. I honestly believe that she's one of the best photographers in the country and it was truly and honor and privilege to work with her on this project. She's the most focused, determined, and professional individual that I've ever worked with. It's my prayer and desire to work with her again on future projects.

I also want to thank every pastor, teacher, and coach that God blessed to touch my life. The lessons that I learned from them about prayer, hard work, discipline, and attention to detail has shaped me into the man that I've become. Without the wisdom of pastors, coaches pushing me to work harder and teachers expecting more out me than I expected from myself, this book and other achievements would never have been possible.

Finally, I want to thank my mother Ella Crutcher for her years of sacrifice and teachings that I will forever be grateful for. I don't have the words to express how much she's meant to any and everything that I've done or will do in this life. There's no way that I could ever repay her, but I want the world to know how much she's appreciated.

DEDICATION

I want to dedicate this book to the loving and everlasting memories of my father James Floyd, my cousin Lamont Porter, and my dear aunt Carol Floyd. These are people that will always be near and dear to my heart. God truly received 3 angels.

INTRODUCTION

One of the great lessons that my parents taught me growing up is that life owes you nothing. Nothing in this world is free and that you need to work for whatever you want in this life. The words and lessons that they gave me were backed up by scripture and the growing pains that life gave me when I tried to live outside of these teachings. All of us middle aged adults went through that "know it all" stage of life in which we later figured out that our parents/grandparents were a lot smarter and wiser than any of us. Some of us were blessed to be given second, third, and more opportunities to straighten out our lives and learn from our mistakes. But there were many that were not so fortunate and had to learn at the expense of their lives or their freedom. I can testify to the fact that I've witnessed friends, family members, and classmates wishing, hoping, and even begging for second chances in life. A few get that "golden" opportunity and make the most of it; but most sadly return right back to the scene of the "crime"

I personally understand that not everyone has had great opportunities in this life to be successful. Not everyone has had access to great educational opportunities or have had the word of God explained to them from a young age. Most didn't understand why their coaches and teachers were "hard" on them in school. Many of them quit before the miracle had a chance to take place in their lives. There are people out there wandering the streets, prisons, shelters, etc. wondering where they went wrong? Wondering if God still loves them? Some are secretly hoping for that second chance.

In this book, I'm going to introduced 6 areas that must be addressed in order for a person to receive spiritual, personal, and professional restoration in their lives. Each chapter will contain lessons and advice based on scripture, philosophy, and time-tested parental guidance. The words are honest, straight forward and no nonsense with the hope that the reader is serious and determined about their next steps in life. It's my hope and prayer that this book will be the beginning, the redemption, or the example needed to bring change into lives and into this world.

Jesus said in Matthew 28:20 (KJV) "Teaching them to observe all things whatsoever I have commanded you."

I sincerely pray and hope that this book will fulfill some of the teaching that Jesus spoke about in the above scripture.

1

CHANGING YOUR SURROUNDINGS

"The greatest discovery of our generation is that human beings can alter their lives by altering their attitudes of mind. As you think so shall you be." William James

1st Corinthians 15:33 ESV: "Do not be deceived. Bad company ruins good morals."

There's a simple truth that Amy Blaschka (2018) wrote about in her piece with for Forbes Magazine. She asks the question: "What corrections would you consciously make to optimize your growth and prepare for a successful future?" The answer to this question is that it starts with awareness and acceptance of a simple truth: **Your environment always wins.**

A person's environment, which includes friends, colleagues, locations, habits, and lifestyle, impact you far more- for better or for worse- than one may realize. We can't make significant, lasting changes, without first altering elements of our environment. Plainly put, when your're trying to grow into the person that you hope to be, it's important and imperative that you surround yourself with individuals that demonstrate those qualities that you aspire to achieve. These people might include pastors from whom you can gain spiritual direction and wisdom, colleagues that encourage you when you get discouraged, or TRUE FRIENDS that will hold you accountable to your goals. I know from experience how difficult that it is to find individuals that see the best in you in spite of your past sins and mistakes. But I can't stress enough how important that it is to have this type of support in your life. Having encouraging people that lift you up and support your dreams will dramatically improve your chances for success.

Of course, on the flip side of the coin, if your environment is inhabited by negative people and influences that are threatened by your choices, then it goes without saying that you'll have a much more difficult time trying to make- let alone maintain- significant changes in your life.

Something else to consider is your habits and lifestyle: are you intentionally placing yourself in situations and locations that will spark or contribute to your growth/change? Or have you (like so many people) fallen into a stagnant comfort zone of the familiar but uninspiring? These are two questions that you should ask yourself each morning before leaving your home. Remember that real growth takes place once we begin to understand whom and what best supports the direction that we want to take and then align ourselves with those people and places that do.

One thing that I want to share and emphasize is that while we're focusing on changing our surroundings, it's important that we change some of our thought process. While it's true that our surroundings can hold us back, so can **REGRETS.** When leaving behind our old surroundings/environments, it's important that we also leave behind the regrets. We have to move into our new surroundings with new and focused thoughts concerning our future and leave our dead weight behind us.

In the King James Version, Luke 9:60 a disciple said, "Let me first go and bury my father." Jesus said to him "Let the dead bury their own dead. But you go and preach the kingdom of God."

When God is pushing you forward, he doesn't want you looking back. He wants your complete focus on the challenges and mission that he's preparing you for. Just like Jesus was preparing the disciple from the above scripture for change, he's doing the same for you. He wants nothing to hold you back and that's exactly what regrets will do. If you spend all your time thinking about the past, you will miss the present and the future. It's important to keep in mind that you can't change what you did or did not do in your past, so **LET IT GO!!**

The only thing you have control over now is how you choose to live your present and future life. Each time that you experience a negative thought about your past, **CHALLENGE IT!!** Don't hold on to it. Refuse to allow these thoughts to have power over your life.

Remember this scripture from Mark 2:22 NLT in which Jesus said "And no one puts new wine into old wineskins. For the wine would burst the wineskins, and the wine and the skins would both be lost. New wine calls for new wineskins."

You can't go into new surroundings holding on to old thoughts and regrets. The two worlds will not be able to survive together. I say again **LET IT GO!!!!**

Know that when you begin this journey into your new surroundings with your new mentality, that you'll most likely begin it alone. You're going to receive all kinds of discouragement, strange looks, and ridicule imaginable. Why? Because people aren't used to seeing your new attitude. People aren't used to having conversations with you about high expectations, change and greatness. A large percentage of individuals are accustomed to "doing just enough to get by." They like their comfort zones and don't want to say or do anything to upset the "apple cart." So yes, it will be a very lonely journey in the beginning. But always remember that the fact that you're receiving all of the above criticisms and treatments is proof that you're on the right path. You're committed to something totally different than those in your surroundings so don't allow the negativity to discourage you. Continue to stay prayerful, stay focused, and stay determined on that straight and narrow path of changing your surroundings. Know that there are many that don't want to see you become successful and will hold you down like the lobsters in the fish tank. Don't waste time becoming angry, frustrated, or resentful towards them because they're only following the attack plan that the "enemy" has against you. He knows when God's about to bless you and wants to do all that he can to discourage or destroy this opportunity. That's why it's important to change your surroundings and get with likeminded individuals that will not only encourage you personally and professionally, but also pray for you spiritually.

When Jesus called his 12 disciples, he took them into new surroundings and removed them from their comfort zones. They were no longer around their families, familiar towns, practicing their professions, or doing any of the things that were familiar to them. Jesus set them a part for his purpose. He instilled in them new mentalities, new purposes, new outlooks, and new determinations. No longer were they simple fishermen, doctors, tax collectors, etc.… They were transformed into disciples and servants of God.

It's this type of transformation that's waiting for those that are also willing to change their surroundings. When Jesus said, "Come and follow me.", he's calling people out from their defeat, drugs, alcohol, misery, laziness, hatred, and other forms of ungodliness in order to transform their lives.

Jesus said in Revelations 21:5 KJV "Behold, I make all things new."

In order for things to be made new, it means that we must let go of the old. The old thoughts, old mentalities, old habits and most importantly the old surroundings must be removed from our lives in order for us to receive the new blessings that God has for us. Will it be easy? Of course not. Challenges weren't meant to be easy. If they were, then everyone would be overcoming challenges in their lives. The main roadblock that people have is that they all say, "It's too hard!" But what they don't realize is that nothing is too hard for God. No challenge is to great that he can't overcome if we just trust and believe in him.

Changing your surroundings will require a great deal of prayer, sacrifice, and faith in the plan that God has for your life. But it's necessary to remove everything and everybody that's been holding you back from receiving what God has for you.

2

LEADERSHIP

James 1:2 NIV "**Blessed is the one who perseveres under trial because, having stood the test, that person will receive the crown of life that the Lord has promised to those who love him.**"

"A true leader has the confidence to stand alone, the courage to make tough decisions, and the compassion to listen to the needs of others." Douglas MacArthur

In MY PERSONAL OPINION, I believe that for any type of change to take place in a person's life, they must have a change in their mentality. That person must be 100% prepared to step out of their "comfort zone" and step onto a deserted island. They must be prepared to sacrifice old friends and even some family members and stand on their own two feet. Living their own lives and doing their own thinking must become the norm every day that God blesses them to wake up.

This is a chapter that I'm dedicating to leadership because I firmly believe that most individuals that are seeking to turn their lives around began as followers. They followed the "popular" crowds, followed the "in" fashions, and eventually followed into spiritual and legal troubles. Many began their smoking, drinking, drugs, and legal troubles by being followers and people pleasers. They never stopped one moment to think of the lifelong consequences that they would face by being a follower. Oh yes, they were given good advice from parents, teachers, coaches, and any other person/group that God sent their way. But because those words didn't come from the "group", they held no significance to the followers.

Until a person is ready to take that next step and become a leader and begin to take control of their life and destiny, change can't be expected. When you make up your mind to transition from a follower to a leader's mentality that's when changes will begin to take place in your life.

How can a person allow others to think for them and yet expect greatness?

How can a person follow the bad habits of others and yet become angry and frustrated when life doesn't turn out the way they envisioned it?

Jesus himself said in Matthew 15:14 "Leave them; they are blind guides. If the blind lead the blind, both will fall into a pit." (NIV)

Even in the midst of our confusion and ignorance, there's a still voice that we hear (most of the time don't listen to) that pleads for us to change our lives. Begs us to make a choice and not follow through with the foolish act. A voice that loves us in spite of the evilness that we may be committing at that time. The man behind this voice turned 12 ordinary men into leaders by using various circumstances in their lives.

Remember it was in Acts 9th chapter that Jesus turned Saul into Paul and made him a leader and disciple in the church.

He took doctors, fishermen, tax collectors, and an eventual traitor and made them "fishers" of men. From the beginning, Jesus has always made a habit of turning nothing into something and he's still doing it today. He's still taking what society calls the lowest of people and making them leaders of men.

He can do the same thing for your life and circumstances. But as I said earlier in the chapter, you have to have a mentality for change and leadership. Your family, spouse, employer, etc. can want it for you all day long. But until you're ready to stand on your own two feet, nothing is going to change.

Based upon my own personal studies of the Bible, it would be my guess that something will cause you to take a deep look at yourself and realize that it's time to take personal responsibility for a change in behavior. Most people before they come upon this revelation, they spent years blaming others or circumstances outside of themselves for not getting what they wanted or needed.

We all have moments of looking outside of ourselves when we should be looking inside. Consider this ladies and gentlemen: The day that you take personal responsibility for managing yourselves is the beginning of hope, happiness, health, and lifelong fulfillment. **AND GREAT LEADERSHIP.**

For most, a change of attitude may be all that's needed to shift from frustration to freedom. This will begin a journey of actually having an impact on your own well-being and those that you **LEAD!!**

Before we truly begin our journey into **leadership**, there are three things that I want you to keep in mind:

1. **People**: Despite your frustrations with others, always remember that you can't change them. They are the only ones that can change themselves.

2. **The Past:** Ladies and Gentlemen the past is done and there isn't anything you can do to change that. Dwelling on miss opportunities, heartbreaks, sins, and mistakes is fruitless. Of course there are things from our past that we can learn from, but staying stuck there will not move people in a positive direction.

3. **The Unknown:** Yes, it's very easy to become stressed about stepping outside of our "comfort zones". But we must realize that the mysteries of the unknown will be revealed with time and patience. Not in our time but in God's time. With faith, people can face the unknown and their futures with the confidence

and understanding that God will reveal needed information in his own time.

Being a leader requires one to become a better human being (and yes this requires change). Part of the journey to becoming a better human being requires one to take a look inside of themselves and learning a new role and also learning one's limitations. Some of the greatest leaders understood that their lives would be an instrument for change within themselves and for the world.

The type of leadership that I want to address in this chapter is known as Authentic Leadership. This is the type of leadership that I personally believe that is needed in abundance in present society. This is an area of leadership that I've researched in abundance over the last 3 years in preparation for my PhD dissertation.

Let me begin by saying that there isn't just one simplified definition of an Authentic Leader. But I will give you 3 viewpoints of this type of leadership.

1. The intrapersonal perspective, which focuses closely on the leader and what goes on within the leader. It incorporates the leader's self-knowledge, self-regulation, and self-concept.

2. The Interpersonal Process outlines authentic leadership as relational, created by leaders and followers together. It results not from the leader's efforts alone, but also from the response of followers.

3. Developmental perspective views authentic leadership as something that can be nurtured in a leader, rather than as a fixed trait. Authentic leadership develops in people over a lifetime and

can be triggered by major life events, such as a severe illness or a new career.

Now that I've given you a little background on authentic leadership, lets look at how this can be used to enhance one's life but also be an example to others.

What I like about authentic leaders is that they have a desire to serve others. Which is the foundation of Jesus's ministry. Jesus said in Matthew 20:28 NIV "Just as the son of man did not come to be served, but to serve, and to give his life as a ransom for many."

Like Jesus, an authentic leader has a real sense of purpose. They know what they are about and where they are going. In addition to knowing their purpose, authentic leaders are inspired and intrinsically motivated about their goals. They are passionate individuals who have a deep-seated interest in what they are doing and truly care about their work. These types of individuals lead by their examples. They are far from perfect and have made their share of mistakes, but those mistakes are now serving as lessons. There's no feeling sorry for themselves and no pity parties. They have laser focus and want change not only for their lives, but also the lives of others.

Authentic leaders understand their own values and behave toward others based on these values. They have a clear idea of who they are, where they are going, and what the right thing is to do. When tested in difficult situations, authentic leaders do not compromise their values, but rather use those situations to strengthen their values.

Self-discipline is another dimension of authentic leadership and is the quality that helps leaders to reach their goals. Self-discipline gives leaders focus and determination. When leaders establish objectives and standards of excellence, self-discipline helps them to reach these goals and to keep everyone accountable. Furthermore, self-discipline gives authentic leaders the energy to carry out their work in accordance with their values. Like long-distance runners, authentic leaders with self-discipline are able to stay focused on their goals. They are able to listen to their inner compass and can discipline themselves to move forward, even in challenging circumstances. In stressful times, self-discipline allows authentic leaders to remain cool, calm, and consistent. Because disciplined leaders are predictable in their behavior, other people know what to expect and find it easier to communicate with them. When the leader is self-directed and "on course," it gives other people a sense of security.

The last characteristic of an authentic leader that I want to address is that of compassion. Compassion and heart are important aspects of authentic leadership. Compassion refers to being sensitive to the plight of others, opening one's self to others, and being willing to help them. Leaders can develop compassion by getting to know others' life stories, doing community service projects, being involved with other racial or ethnic groups, or traveling to developing countries. These activities increase the leader's sensitivity to other cultures, backgrounds, and living situations.

With this chapter on **LEADERSHIP,** I'm challenging the readers to find out what they're made of. Anybody can spend their lives as a follower. But in order for there to be significant change in the mind, body, and spirit a person has to take the journey of Peter out on the water. They must trust God through the storms and waves and never take their eyes off him.

The Bible teaches in 1st John 4:1-5 NIV "But try the spirit whether they are of God" In order for follower to develop into a leader, they must step out on the waters of faith and understand that people will talk about them. People will gossip and lie on them. People will say all manner of evil against them. They should not let that discourage them but understand that the enemy is simply doing his job. He's going to do all that he can to discourage the change because of the large numbers of people that will be blessed from the newfound leadership.

Look at the lives of Moses, David, and Joseph of the old testament as examples. How the enemy fought against them becoming leaders because he knew that their LEADERSHIP would BLESS thousands.

As a child, my mother would always tell me "Son never sell yourself short because you never know what God has in store for you." I say the same to the readers to never sell yourselves short. Live for God, think for yourselves, and resist to the temptation of living your lives as followers.

Because I consider this of great importance, I'm going to leave you with what I feel are the five basic characteristics of leadership. It is my prayer that you learn and adapt these characteristics to your own lives.

(1) they have a strong sense of purpose,

(2) they have strong values about the right thing to do,

(3) they establish trusting relationships with others,

(4) they demonstrate self-discipline and act on their values, and

(5) they are sensitive and empathetic to the plight of others

3

WORK ETHIC

Colossians 3:23 ESV "Whatever you do, work heartily, as for the Lord and not for men"

"Talent is a gift, but your attitude, work ethic, and character are things that you have to develop yourself." Rebekah Harkness

"It always seems impossible until it's done" Nelson Mandela

KOBE BRYANT ONCE SAID "I have nothing in common with lazy people who blame others for their lack of success. Great things come from hard work and perseverance. NO EXCUSES!!"

Michael Jordan once said "Obstacles don't have to stop you. If you run into a wall, don't turn around and give up. Figure out how to climb it, go through it, or work around it."

I truly thank God that I came up during a time in which parents instilled a strong work ethic in their children. Whether it was cutting grass, raking leaves, washing the family car, or washing dishes there were always a set of chores to be completed around the house. Not only would they need to be completed, but they would need to be completed correctly. If not, then there were always consequences to pay. For example, there would be a loss of phone privileges, no television, no playing outside with friends, and possibly the loss of driving privileges.

These things seemed very harsh during our childhood, but they taught us valuable lessons. Lessons such as the value of a dollar and the rewards of hard work and discipline. The trials and tribulation of these lessons developed work ethics for our adult lives.

As children we would often hear the words "Hard work never killed anybody." These words were like seeds that were being planted and watered each day of our childhood. There was never any mention of an "easy" way out or "get rich quick schemes". There was no whining or complaining and we were held responsible for completing tasks/chores in a certain amount of time.

As Archie and Edith Bunker used to sing "Those were the days." Those were the days that I experienced in my childhood. Days that built character and a strong work ethic that aren't taught very much in the present generation. Unfortunately, these lessons aren't being passed down like they once were. Because of this, we're seeing an increasing number of kids dropping out of school, employees quitting jobs when it gets to hard, increases in "get rich quick schemes", lack of motivation to excel, and an over "quitters mentality".

We're seeing a vast decrease of people being held accountable for their work ethics (or lack thereof). Very few people are looking deep within themselves to find out what they're made of. Even fewer individuals care to challenge themselves to overcome obstacles in their lives. Have we forgotten the words of Frederick Douglas "If there is no struggle there is no progress" How can a person expect to push forward in their lives if they hold on to a "just enough to get by mentality"?

Your success in this life will go only as far as your work ethic will take you.

Allow me to share with you my personal definition of work ethic.

A strong work ethic is an important part of being successful in your personal and professional life. Work ethic is a set of values based on the ideals of discipline and hard work. Building a strong work ethic will allow a person to train themselves so that hard work is almost automatic. Forming good habits such as focusing, staying motivated, finishing tasks immediately, and more helps to create a good work ethic that will be a shining example to friends, family, and fellow employees.

If you put in the work, the rewards and changes will come. Hold on. Let me change that. If you **CONSISTENTLY** put in the work, rewards and changes will come. You have to give 100% each and every day. Even when you fall short of your goals, be willing to pick yourself back up and go at it even harder. "Leaving it all on the floor" will keep you from having any regrets or excuses. How many times have you heard someone say, "If only I didn't quit 20 years ago, where would I be today" Think about that for a moment because that person is trying to tell you that quitting will cause a lifetime of regret. If you quit once, you'll spend the rest of your life quitting because it'll become a habit. Also ask yourself these questions: What will you accomplish by quitting? What will you gain? Give those questions due consideration before you entertain the thought of giving up on your goals.

Here are two characteristics of people with strong work ethics:

1. People with a good work ethic have the ability to stay focused on tasks for as long as necessary to get them done. Building persistence will allow you to basically train yourself to work for longer periods of time while also working harder.

2. People with a strong work ethic do not procrastinate and instead immediately tackle their work tasks. In addition to getting to tasks right away, a good work ethic involves doing things properly.

In order for any type of change or success to come into your life, you have to be willing to work hard, sacrifice, and dedicate yourself to never quit until a task is done. No matter how long it takes, no matter what friends you may lose, and no matter what you may miss out on never quit until a job is done. It may be difficult, but always remember that repetition becomes a habit. The more that you practice something, the more it becomes a part of you. Your work ethic is what people are going to know you by.

Always remember that complacency is the enemy of success. Never rest on your laurels. Always work harder to be better the next day and the day after that. Understand that even with a strong work ethic, there's going to be days of failure. Days that you'll fall short. But don't let those days discourage you; instead, turn them into motivation. Turn your weaknesses into your strengths and make your strengths even greater. In other words, NEVER BE SATISFIED!!!

Greatness doesn't come from satisfaction. It comes from striving to be the best that you can be every day that God Blesses you to wake up. Always stay prayerful, stay focused and stay determined. Your reward may not come today or tomorrow. But if you keep working hard and improving your work ethic, you'll receive your reward. Repeated dominance doesn't happen without hard work—without the understanding that you can't get what you want with effort and determination. That "competitive enthusiasm" that never-say-die mentality, is vital to your success. Not just when it supposedly matters, but all the time—because it matters all the time.

Psalms 128:2 ESV "You shall eat the fruit of the labor of your hands; you shall be blessed, and it shall be well with you.

4

RELATIONSHIPS/ MARRIAGE

Genesis 2:24 ESV "Therefore a man shall leave his father and his mother and hold fast to his wife, and they shall become one flesh."

1st Peter 4:8 NIV "Above all, love each other deeply, because love covers a multitude of sins."

"A successful marriage requires falling in love many times, always with the same person."
Mignon Mclaughlin

From the beginning, in Genesis 2:18 NIV, the Lord himself said:

"It's not good for man to be alone. I will make a helper suitable for him."

Then the Lord went on further to say in Genesis 2:24 NIV

"This is why a man leaves his father and mother and is united to his wife and they become one flesh."

From the beginning, the Lord established marriage as a lifetime contract. It was never meant to end after 6 months, 6 years, or even 60 years. That was never by God's design. Marriage was established to be a lifetime commitment. If we simply think about the vows that are exchanged during a wedding ceremony, it would be obvious the magnitude of the commitment that God is establishing between 2 people.

Take a moment to repeat this to yourself:

"For better or for worse

In sickness and health

For rich or poor

In good times and bad times

For as long as you both shall live"

This is what 2 people are promising each other before God and witnesses, These vows are also representing a lifelong commitment. That's why it's important to be 100% sure and ready before entering into the HOLY

BONDS OF MATIROMONY. We need to remember and realize that God's word holds us to higher standards than the promises of society. Society teaches that divorce is a natural progression and that a lack of commitment is ok. It also teaches that making excuses and breaking promises/commitments is also acceptable. More and more society is teaching that its ok for a person's word to be worthless (It was once taught that a man's word was his bond. When is the last time that you've heard that?)

I personally believe that we are living in a time in which the importance of marriage and the HOLY BONDS OF MATRIMONY aren't being taught nor are there many great examples for younger generations to follow. One can make an argument that maybe the lack of examples and education is attributing to the nearly 50% divorce rate that our nation carries. Maybe if we're not only taught, but also see better examples of the commitment to vows, then perhaps people would obtain a better understanding of the level of commitment in maintaining God's lifetime contract (marriage).

From a definition standpoint, marriage is defined as a gift from God, one that should not be taken for granted. It is the right atmosphere to engage in sexual relations and to build a family life. Getting married in a church, in front of God, is very important. Why? Because a marriage is a public declaration of love and commitment. It's two people telling the world that they will love each other forever. It's also a pastor telling witness that "Therefore what God has joined together, let no man put asunder." In other words, man has no right separating or even attempting to separate God's HOLY UNION.

As CHRISTIANS, we're supposed to know better!!

But there is a truth that we have to deal with in today's society. A truth that we as Christians must learn in order for our marriages/relationships to be a better example for the world to view and learn from. The truth is that although God's marriage calls for a lifetime commitment, no relationship comes with lifetime guarantees. As a divorced man, I can further testify that even those of us that attend church and confess Christ as our Lord and savior can have marriages that fall apart.

Of course, as Christians we know that applying Biblical principles to our marriages will give us a stronger foundation. But the question is: What are we doing about it? Are we making the daily effort to apply these principles to God's Holy Union?

But here's something that we as Christians should begin to think about concerning our marriages:

According to author Gary Thomas, we're not asking the right questions. What if your relationship isn't as much about you and your spouse as it is about you and God?

Instead of asking why we have struggles in the first place, the more important issue is how we deal with them. Because ladies and gentlemen every marriage is going to have struggles. Every marriage is going to have their trials and tribulations. That's why God has us to make vows in the beginning so that we understand that we're committed to stand by our spouses when we face those struggles. Of course, the vows don't instruct us how to deal with them, but "I do" means that one way or another we'll figure it out together.

In Thomas's book titled: Sacred Marriage (I highly recommend married couples facing struggles to read this) Thomas has not written your typical "how to have a happier relationship" book. Rather, he asks: How can we use the challenges, joys, struggles and celebrations of marriage to draw closer to God? What if God designed marriage to make us both happy *and* holy?

Now that's something that most of us haven't thought about. But think about this for a moment:

In this midst of our struggles, who do we call on? God

When facing trials and tribulations, who do we call on? God

He didn't design marriages to be solved by judges and divorce attorneys. God wants us to give all the struggles to him that we can't handle in order for HOLINESS AND HAPPINESS to be restored.

But more on that a little later.

Right now, let's take a look at some realistic expectations of marriage that will help us in our approach to spouses.

The first thing that we should do from a spiritual standpoint is we have to stop asking of marriage what God never designed it to give — perfect happiness, conflict-free living, and idolatrous obsession.

Instead, we should appreciate what God designed marriage to provide: partnership, spiritual intimacy, and the ability to pursue God — together.

Understand that everyone has bad days, yells at his or her spouse or is downright selfish. Despite these imperfections, God created the husband and wife to steer each other in His direction. Marriage is yet another example in which we were created to serve him.

For example, when a husband/wife forgives each other from an argument, it's how they should learn to accept God's forgiveness and acceptance also (remember it all goes back to giving him the glory). Forgiveness is a great example of God's grace and mercy. If he can forgive us and wipe our slates clean, then how much more should we do it for our husbands/wives?

One thing that I sit back and watch is the growing "me-centered" world that we're living in and can understand why marriage is so heavily attacked. As I said in the beginning of the chapter, marriage is a gift from God and so therefore that makes it a HOLY UNION. Anything that's HOLY is centered around God and not the selfish ambitions of man.

Here are 4 things to keep in mind when we're thinking about God's Holy Union:

- God created marriage as a loyal partnership between one man and one woman.
- Marriage is the firmest foundation for building a family.
- God designed sexual expression to help married couples build intimacy.
- Marriage mirrors God's covenant relationship with His people.

In this "me-centered" world that we live in, it's important to remember that marriage is about what you can do for each other and not individual needs. It's not about how much money a man has in his bank account, how good/bad the spouse performs sexually, fat/skinny, etc... It's about a loyal partnership between husband and wife. What's the definition of loyalty? It's a strong feeling of support or allegiance. Remember that the next time you think of abandoning your spouse. Because God's purpose for marriage extends far beyond our desire for personal happiness. I genuinely believe that God did not create marriage just to give us a pleasant means of repopulating the world and providing a steady societal institution to raise children. Further, he planted marriage among humans yet another signpost pointing to His own eternal, spiritual existence.

I said it earlier, we are here to serve him.

If happiness is our primary goal, we'll get a divorce as soon as happiness seems to wane. If receiving love is our primary goal, we'll dump our spouse as soon as they seem to be less attentive. But if we marry for the glory of God, to model His love and commitment to our children, and to reveal His witness to the world, divorce makes no sense.

In my research and observations, I've learned that couples who've survived a potentially marriage-ending situation, such as infidelity or a life-threatening disease, may continue to battle years of built-up resentment, anger, or bitterness. So, what are some ways to strengthen a floundering relationship — or even encourage a healthy one?

Here are four suggestions:

- Focus on your spouse's strengths rather than their weaknesses.
- Encourage rather than criticize.
- Pray for your spouse instead of gossiping about them.
- Learn and live what Christ teaches about relating to and loving others.

Young couples in particular can benefit from this advice. After all, many newlyweds aren't adequately prepared to make the transition from seeing one another several times a week to suddenly sharing *everything*. Odds are annoying habits and less-than-appealing behaviors will surface. Yet as Christians, we are called to respect everyone — especially our spouse.

In closing, I want to add that marriage/relationships will truly challenge a man/woman and test their Christianity. We make the mistake of listening to everyone but the man/woman that God has placed in our lives. It's important to recognize that not everyone wants your marriage to succeed and so that's an even greater reason to put your trust in the Lord. Pray and consult the word before consulting any outside sources. Nobody understands you or your marriage better than God and so therefore look to him for the solutions to your problems; unless God leads you to others for advice and solutions. With a Christ-centered relationship, positive-centered attitude and an unwavering commitment to making it work, your marriage can flourish — just as God designed.

5

LOVING EACH OTHER/ DISCRIMINATION

Galatians 3:28 ESV "There is neither Jew nor Greek, there is neither slave nor free, there is no male and female, for you are all one in Christ Jesus."

Galatians 5:14 ESV For the whole law is fulfilled in one word: "You shall love your neighbor as yourself."

There's so much hatred and discrimination in the world today. People hating one another based on their culture, skin color, political affiliations, and any other reason that they can think of. We're seeing more protests, police violence, property destruction, and division than at any time in modern history. Murders and kidnappings are on the rise and people seem to grow more cold hearted by the day.

It's truly a sad time in history. We live under a theme "One nation under God" but it seems that we've lost touch with the Christian values that our nation was built on. We've forgotten that "In God We Trust" is not just a national slogan, but it's also a lifestyle.

How can we as Christians attend church on Sunday but hate our brothers and sisters on Monday based on any form of discrimination? Where does God any where from Genesis to Revelation say that one race is more superior than another race? Where does God give us the authority to pass laws that grants advantages for one race over another? The ultimate question is: Where did God give the authority to hate our fellowman? Didn't Jesus himself say to "Love one another as I have loved you"? "Do unto others as you would have them do unto you."

So, if these verses and scriptures are taught on a weekly basis from birth to adulthood and from generation to generation, then why doesn't that materialize into a more loving and unified society? Why are we continuing to discriminate when we've learned about the love of Jesus Christ?

The fact of the matter is that just like biblical principles can be taught, so can discrimination.

How do we know this?

A baby comes into the world not knowing anything about skin color, hatred, or bigotry. But at some point, between their birth and the time they reach adulthood, they're either taught to love everyone or just love everyone with the same skin pigmentation as you. Even though these same children attended church and learned the scriptures, they were taught a different type of lifestyle when they're among their family. The reason that I say family is because during my 12 years in school I never encountered any teacher that taught one race of kids to look at another any differently. We studied, played, fought, and even walked to school together. But at no time was our education compromised simply because of the color of our skin.

So if values of discrimination weren't taught in the school, then the only other place would be the home. Just like Christian values are passed down by generations, so is discrimination.

Unlike in the pre–civil rights era, when racial prejudice and discrimination were overt and widespread, today discrimination is less readily identifiable, posing problems for social scientific conceptualization and measurement. There are various areas in which discrimination has become persistent but is often "slide under the rug." For example, racial inequality in employment, housing, and other social domains has renewed interest in the possible role of discrimination. We must be aware that racial discrimination refers to unequal treatment of persons or groups based on their race or ethnicity. It also incudes decisions and processes that may not themselves have any explicit racial content but that have the consequence of producing or reinforcing racial disadvantage.

Now that we understand that there's a problem and the definition of the problem, the question becomes: How can changes be made? What must people of all races do in order to bring unity and love among God's people?

I truly believe that there is a cure against discrimination. The deep wounds can be healed but the healing process is intricate, deliberate and will require involvement from those who have previously remained silent. When racism discrimination raises its ugly head, silence becomes toxic and our apathy is interpreted as total acceptance. We always have a choice: do nothing and let discrimination go uncontested and flourish, or do something -- act up, rise up, and speak up. We must pick up the armor of righteousness daily in order to slay the evil forces of discrimination at work against us. It will not be easy and it will not always be comfortable for any of us but courage is a game changer. We must each take a step each day to garner support and find our voice as the moral majority.

Here are 10 steps that I feel can help people of all races and nationalities step out of the silence:

1. Learn about other people and their culture but go beyond foods and festivals.

2. Explore the unfamiliar. Put yourself in situations where you are in the visible minority.

3. Be a proactive parent. Talk to your children candidly about race.

4. Don't tell or laugh at stereotypical jokes.

5. Think before you speak. Words can hurt whether you mean them to or not.

6. Be a role model and help educate others regarding your own experiences.

7. Don't make assumptions because they are usually wrong, and stereotypes are destructive.

8. Consider how race and racism impact your life and those around you.

9. Don't let others get away with biased language or behavior- speak up and out.

10. Take a position against hate and take a Stand Against Racism.

Hate attacks civility, community and escalates into the disease of discrimination -- discrimination hurts everyone.

It's truly important to make a stand. As the old saying goes, "saying and doing nothing is part of the problem." We must make every effort to bring people together in conversation and begin to learn from each other. Make an effort to learn about other cultures and languages. Let's get out of the "Me" mindset and expand our minds and horizons beyond our own neighborhoods.

God created us all unique and different. We are not all meant to be the same. Each culture has something to offer the world and one is no better than the other.

Keep in mind that we will all stand before the same God and be judged in the same manner regardless of the color of our skin or our nationality.

Change begins in each one of us. The late great Michael Jackson once said "I'm talking about the man in the mirror. I'm asking him to change his ways. If you want to make the world a better place, take a look at yourself and make a change."

That's what's going to have to happen if we're to restore some sort of love and unity in the world. We must wake up every morning and take a hard look at ourselves. We must ask: Am I part of the problem or am I going to be part of the solution? Am I going to point fingers and blame others, or am I going to be the example that the world is needing? The world needs to see more people practicing what they preach. We've seen enough "lip service" and excuses. If a person truly has the Christ living inside of them, then they will live as an example of love and stand against the hatred of discrimination. Again, I ask: How can we say amen on Sunday but then say I hate you on Monday? Is that the example that Christ left is disciples?

Matthew 28:18-20 NIV Jesus told the disciples:

"All authority in heaven and on earth has been given to me. Go therefore and make disciples of ALL nations, baptizing them in the name of the father, son and Holy Spirit, and teaching them to obey EVERYTHING that I have commanded you."

The above scripture is one of many examples in which Jesus teaches us not to discriminate. He loves us all equally and wants all nations to be taught the fruits of his word. We must approach each other in the same manner. Understanding that ALL of God's word is for ALL of his people. That means that one person or nation is no better than the other. We have no right to discriminate in any way. If we're teaching all that Jesus has commanded, then that means LOVE has to be a part of that teaching. And if we're teaching and living in LOVE, then how can we desire segregation based upon the color of one's skin?

The Good news known as the Gospel doesn't just mean that we're brought near to God. It also means we're brought near to the people we once considered so different from ourselves. God restores our relationships with people and groups we've mistreated. That's called reconciliation: the removal of prejudice and the restoration of a relationship to healthy understanding and appreciation for each other.

God is a reconciling God. The Gospel is, at its core, a message of reconciliation.

God brings peace where there was once strife, and kindness where there was once animosity. He's done it with us, and He can do it between us and our neighbors—whether black, white, Latino, or otherwise.

If we belong to Jesus, we are part of His movement to bring more reconciliation between people and God, As His disciples, we have the opportunity to share how the life-changing message of the Gospel creates a healthy relationship with God and healthy relationships between people, no matter who they are.

Your job and my job, as we learn to follow Jesus step by step, includes reconciliation because the message of Jesus is that we all belong with God, together—no separation, no difference in status or worth.

6
VALUES AND PRINCIPLES

Matthew 6:24 ESV "No one can serve two masters, for either he will hate the one and love the other, or he will be devoted to the one and despise the other. You cannot serve God and money.

Proverbs 19:1 ESV "Better is a poor person who walks in his integrity than one who is crooked in speech and is a fool."

"Stand up for what you believe in, even if it means standing alone." Kim Hanks

I CAN REMEMBER AS A CHILD getting up early on Saturday mornings to catch those Looney Tunes. I'd always love to hear Yosemite Sam say "Well that's against my principles, but I'll do it."

You had to have grown up during that period or before to understand the importance of a man's principles. Principles were what the man lived by. It was a code of honor that defined who he was as a person.

A person of principle *means* someone who faithfully follows their principle or set of principles rather than abandoning them when convenient. If faced with a seemingly difficult decision in life, he or she will refer to his or her guiding set of principles and then merely deduce the correct action from it. If on rare occasions such principled people do not behave according to their principles, they would consider such actions to be moral mistakes on their part.

A Christian would certainly strive to be a person of principle. Such a person would live his or her life according to the moral guidelines set out in the Bible; especially for instance the Ten Commandments. Suppose Norbert, a Christian, really wants to get his son a wristwatch from the local department store but cannot afford to pay for it. He is quite certain that he could steal the watch without being caught. To resolve his inner dispute, all he has to do is refer to his set of guiding principles, and he will recall that "Thou shalt not steal" applies. Norbert, being a man of principle, leaves the store disappointed, without the watch, but also without having violated his principle, and therefore without having acted immorally.

Our values and principles are important because they help us to grow and develop. They help us to create the future we want to experience. The decisions we make are a reflection of our values and beliefs, and they are always directed towards a specific purpose. That purpose is the satisfaction of our individual or collective (organizational) needs. *WHEN WE USE OUR VALUES TO MAKE DECISIONS, WE MAKE A DELIBERATE CHOICE TO FOCUS ON WHAT IS IMPORTANT TO US*

When the things that you do and the way you behave match your values, life is usually good – you're satisfied and content. But when these don't align with your personal values, that's when things feel... wrong. This can be a real source of unhappiness.

Therefore, making a conscious effort to identify your values is so important. Like the example of Yosemite Sam that I used at the beginning of this chapter. For all of his anger and faults, he understood his values and principles.

Because values and principles aren't being taught in the home as they once were, I think it's important to dedicate a small chapter to what I consider rather important areas. Areas that I believe gives a person's life meaning and purpose.

Let's take a closer look!!

Values and principles exist, whether you recognize them or not. Life can be much easier when you acknowledge your values – and when you make plans and decisions that honor them.

If you value family, but you have to work 70-hour weeks in your job, will you feel internal stress and conflict? And if you don't value competition, and you work in a highly competitive sales environment, are you likely to be satisfied with your job?

In these types of situations, understanding your principles and values can really help. When you know your own values, you can use them to make decisions about how to live your life, and you can answer questions like these:

- What job should I pursue?
- Should I accept this promotion?
- Should I start my own business?
- Should I compromise, or be firm with my position?
- Should I follow tradition, or travel down a new path?

So, take the time to understand the real priorities in your life, and you'll be able to determine the best direction for you and your life goals!!

As I said earlier, these areas will give a person's life definition and meaning. You'll be your own person and do your own thinking. Your decisions will be based on what you're made of and the spirit inside of you. You'll follow your mind and not worldly trends.

Here's a little advice to think about if you're still trying to find your values and principles:

Values are usually fairly stable, yet they don't have strict limits or boundaries. Also, as you move through life, your values may change. For example, when you start your career, success – measured by money and status – might be a top priority. But after you have a family, work-life balance may be what you value more.

As your definition of success changes, so do your personal values. Therefore, keeping in touch with your values is a lifelong exercise. You should continuously revisit this, especially if you start to feel unbalanced... and you can't quite figure out why.

Keep in mind that when you're trying to define your values and principles, you discover what's tremendously important to you. A good way of starting to do this is to look back on your life – to identify when you felt really good, and really confident that you were making good choices.

Here are a few steps and questions that will help you along the way:

Step 1: Identify the times when you were happiest

Find examples from both your career and personal life. This will ensure some balance in your answers.

- What were you doing?

- Were you with other people? Who?
- What other factors contributed to your happiness?

Step 2: Identify the times when you were most proud

Use examples from your career and personal life.

- Why were you proud?
- Did other people share your pride? Who?
- What other factors contributed to your feelings of pride?

Step 3: Identify the times when you were most fulfilled and satisfied

Again, use both work and personal examples.

- What need or desire was fulfilled?

- How and why did the experience give your life meaning?
- What other factors contributed to your feelings of fulfillment?

Identifying and understanding your values and principles is a challenging and important exercise. Your personal values are a central part of who you are – and who you want to be. By becoming more aware of these important factors in your life, you can use them as a guide to make the best choice in any situation.

Some of life's decisions are really about determining what you value most. When many options seem reasonable, it's helpful and comforting to rely on your principles and values – and use them as a strong guiding force to point you in the right direction.

It's not always going to be easy to live by our principles and values because sometimes life gets in the way. We get sidetracked and sometimes we're going to fail. Keep in mind that's just a normal part of life. It happens!! Don't sit in a corner and dwell on it because as God has said many times in his word, "We all have sinned and fallen short of his glory."

Think about it like this: Have you ever been in any of these situations?

- Someone said or did something that you strongly disagreed with, but you didn't speak up about it and felt ashamed afterwards.
- You set goals for yourself and then failed to meet them.
- Your life or career haven't worked out the way you wanted them to.

- What you want often clashes with what you've got to do or what's "practical."
- You're so busy pleasing other people that you're not even sure what your own true values are.

If any of these have ever happened to you (and I'm sure that they have), then consider yourself human but not a failure. Just because we fall short on something doesn't mean that we're a failure nor does it mean that we should give up (like a large percentage of people do. Those are the ones that never move forward in this life). It means that we pick ourselves back up and continue to live by our values and principles.

Too many people think that the "grass looks greener" on the other side and forget about what they stand for. They forget about all those years they worked hard and sacrificed to live by their values and principles. One moment of weakness can ruin a great reputation that you worked hard to build up.

So again, remember just because you stumble doesn't mean that you're a failure. It just might mean that you should learn and grow from your mistakes.

When you live by your values and principles, you feel better about yourself and are more focused on doing the things that are important to you. Everybody is different, and what makes one person happy may leave another person feeling anxious or disengaged. Defining your personal values and then living by them can help you to feel more fulfilled and to make choices that make *you* happy, even if they don't make sense to other people.

Yes, you'll have some conflict with family and friends when it comes to living by your principles and values. You may value creativity, but you've got family members to take care of, so you can't take the risk of embarking on an art career. Or you may value honesty but feel that there are certain lies you need to tell in order to preserve important relationships, to keep your job, or whatever else.

These are important barriers, and they're worth reflecting on seriously. But it's also worth remembering that there are many ways to live your values, and you don't have to reject all compromises and ignore practical considerations.

If your values and principles come into conflict with those of others or the wider society, you may face some difficulties, but you can still live with integrity in your own life. If your circumstances allow, you can also fight to change society according to your own beliefs. Look at many of the heroes of history like Susan B. Anthony or Martin Luther King, Jr., and you'll find people whose personal values came into conflict with those of their time. But if you don't feel ready for that kind of struggle, then you could choose to focus on your own actions and on living according to your own values, without challenging those around you who live differently.

7
FINAL WORDS

Philippians 4:6-7 NIV "Do not be anxious about anything, but in every situation, by prayer and petition, with thanksgiving, present your requests to God. And the peace of God, which transcends all understanding, will guard your hearts and your minds in Christ Jesus."

If we truly want change in our lives, it's going to come through prayer, hard work, dedication, and determination. Nobody is going to be able to do it for you nor is there some magic "quick fix" formula for this to happen. You're going to have to wake up one day with a burning desire for a better life and goals that you want to achieve. You're going to have to want it so bad, that you think about nothing else over the course of a 24-hour period.

It's going to mean accepting every challenge and overcoming every obstacle that the enemy puts in your way. Crying, failure, and excuses will no longer be options as your focus will be on whatever you're trying to achieve. The gossip, the backbiting, and doubters will be used for motivation. The more they talk and doubt your new direction, will make you work that much harder.

Yes, you'll lose friends and even family members along the way because your values and principles have changed. Your vocabulary and habits no longer coincide with theirs and this will eventually leave you on an island all alone. There will be nobody but you and God. He'll probably be the only person that believes in you and understand the blood, sweat, and tears that you'll be shedding along the way. If you remember there were many occasions that Jesus had to get off to himself in order to talk to God and recharge his spirit. In the Garden of Gethsemane, when Jesus went away from his disciples to pray and the agony that he experienced ,was an example of what we must face when we decide to accept the will of God for our lives and move away from people.

When we make this decision, that's when we begin to listen to that spirit within and find out exactly what we're made of. In Luke 17:21 KJV Jesus said, "The kingdom of God is inside of us." That's something very powerful. Once we call on what's inside of us to change our lives and direction, it causes a powerful move that most people around us can't understand. People will be able to see you, but they won't be able to understand the move that God is causing inside.

So, as you continue on your new journey, keep in mind how the disciples and others abandoned Jesus after he was captured. He had to make that journey alone.

Same as you.

Don't get angry or discouraged when people abandon you because it's a journey that you'll also have to make alone. God needs to "clean" you up from the inside out. It might take months, or it could take years but stay the course. Let God have his perfect work as he prepares you for a new course in life.

My prayer is that God blesses each person that reads this book with love, peace, and understanding. In order for change to come in our lives and this world, we must remember that God is the beginning and the ending. The first and the last.